# Disney POP★ROCK FOR TEENS

ISBN-13: 978-1-4234-1296-0
ISBN-10: 1-4234-1296-6

**Wonderland Music Company, Inc.**

**Walt Disney Music Company**

In Australia Contact:
Hal Leonard Australia Pty. Ltd.
4 Lentara Court
Cheltenham, Victoria, 3192 Australia
Email: ausadmin@halleonard.com

DISTRIBUTED BY

**HAL•LEONARD®**
CORPORATION

7777 W. BLUEMOUND RD. P.O. BOX 13819 MILWAUKEE, WI 53213

Visit Hal Leonard Online at www.halleonard.com

# ON THE CD . . .

**Allison Blackwell**

Featured in major productions of *Caroline or Change*, *Hairspray*, *Ragtime*, *Aida*, *Jesus Christ Superstar*, and *Dreamgirls*. Performed in Walt Disney Tributes to Chita Rivera, Diahann Carroll, and Louis Gossett, Jr.

**Sarah Jane Everman**

Broadway: *The Apple Tree* (covering Eve, Barbara and Passionella), *Wicked* (US Glinda), and *Wonderful Town*. Most recently seen as Kathy Selden in the Goodspeed Opera House production of *Singin' in the Rain*.

**Niki Scalera**

Attended NYU Tisch School. Most recently on Broadway in Disney's *Tarzan*. Featured in the Las Vegas production of *We Will Rock You* (Queen) and toured in *Footloose*. Appeared in the Emmy nominated *Don't Touch*.

Producer **Michael Dansicker** has worked as arranger, composer, musical director and pianist on over 100 Broadway and Off-Broadway productions; from *Grease* (1975) to *Series of Dreams* (Tharp/Dylan Project '05.) His musical *Twenty Fingers, Twenty Toes* (Book, Music and Lyrics) has been performed Off-Broadway at the NY WPA Theatre and The York and his Boogie-Woogie Opera *Swing Shift* was performed at the Manhattan Theatre Club. He has composed original music for over a dozen plays in New York, including The *Glass Menagerie* (revival with Jessica Tandy) and *Total Abandon* (with Richard Dreyfus), and musically supervised the Royal Shakespeare Company transfers of *Piaf*, *Good*, and *Les Liasons Dangereuses*. He served as vocal consultant to the hit films *Elf* (New Line Cinema), *Analyze That!* (Warner Bros.), and *Meet the Parents* (Universal), and also scored the dance sequences for Paramount's comedy classic *Brain Donors* (starring John Turturro). In the world of concert dance, he has composed and scored pieces for Twyla Tharp, American Ballet Theatre, Geoffrey Holder, Mikhail Baryshnikov, and The Joffrey, as well as serving as pianist to Jerome Robbins and Agnes Demille. Michael currently works as creative consultant to Walt Disney Entertainment. For Hal Leonard Corporation, he composed the music for *The Audition Suite* (lyrics by Martin Charnin) and compiled the four books of The *16-Bar Theatre Audition* series, as well as producing many vocal tracks. As a vocal coach, he works with the top talent in New York and Hollywood (including Sony's pop division). As audition pianist, he works regularly with important casting directors on both coasts, and for 15 years has played all major auditions for Jay Binder, the "dean" of Broadway casting. Mr. Dansicker's original music is licensed by BMI. He holds a MA from the Catholic University of America.

# CONTENTS

*Singers on the CD:*
**Allison Blackwell** (tracks 1, 8), **Sarah Jane Everman** (tracks 2, 3, 6),
**Niki Scalera** (tracks 4, 5, 7, 9, 10)

Vocal recordings produced by Michael Dansicker
Engineered by Chip Fabrizi at P.P.I. Recording, Inc., New York City
Instrumental tracks produced by Artemis.

# I WON'T SAY
## (I'm in Love)
### from Walt Disney Pictures' *Hercules*

Music by Alan Menken
Lyrics by David Zippel

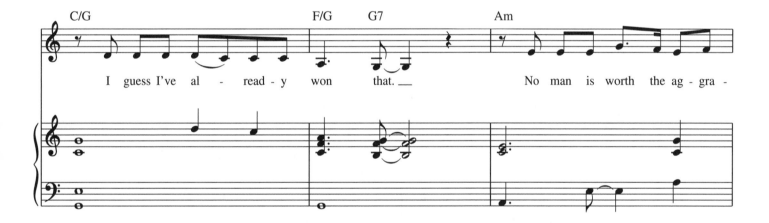

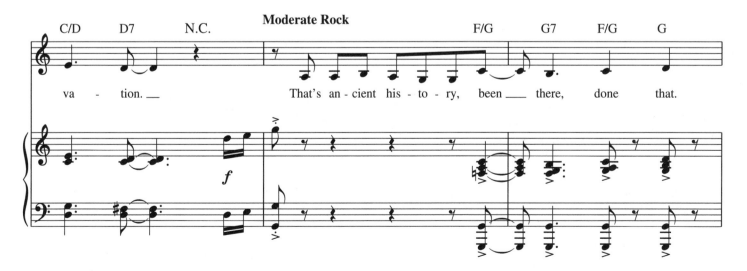

Who d'ya think you're kid-din', he's ___ the Earth and heav-en to you. Try to keep it hid-den, hon-

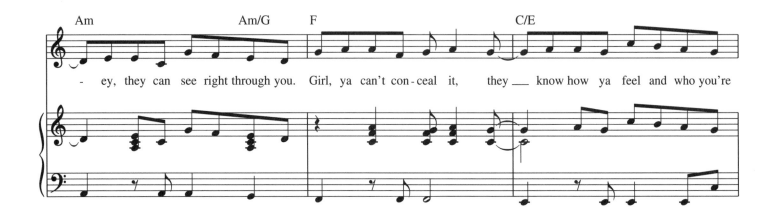

-ey, they can see right through you. Girl, ya can't con-ceal it, they ___ know how ya feel and who you're

think - ing of. ___ Oh. ___ No chance, ___ no way, ___

___ I won't say ___ it, no, no. You swoon, ___ you sigh, ___ why de-ny ___ it, uh oh. ___

It's too __ cli - ché, __ I won't say __ I'm in love.

I thought my heart had learned its les - son. __ It feels so good when you start _____ out. __

My head is scream-ing, get a grip, girl, _ un-less you're dy-ing to cry __ your heart _ out.

You keep on de - ny - ing who __ you are and how you're feel-ing. Ba - by they're not buy-ing, hon, _

_____ they saw ya hit the ceil-ing. Face it like a grown-up, when _____ ya gon-na own up that ya

got, got it, got it bad. _____ Woh. _____ No chance, _ no way, _ I won't say _ it, no,

no. Give up, _ give in. _ Check the grin, you're in love. This scene _ won't play, _ I won't say _ I'm in

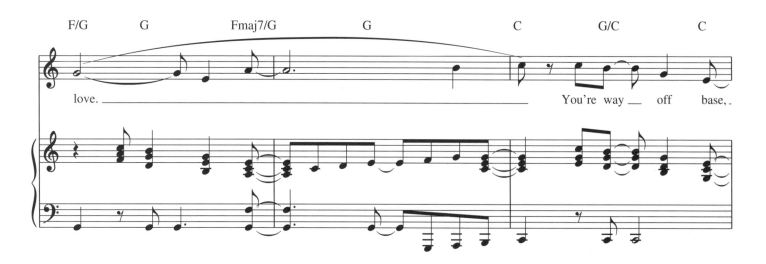

love. _____ You're way _ off base,

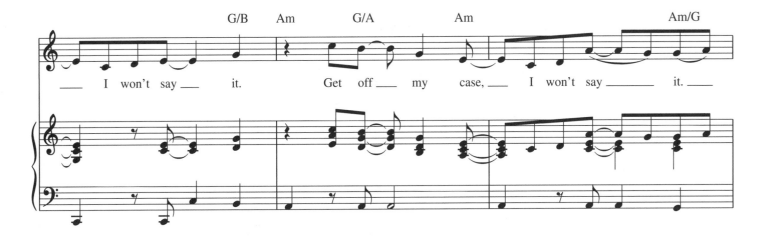

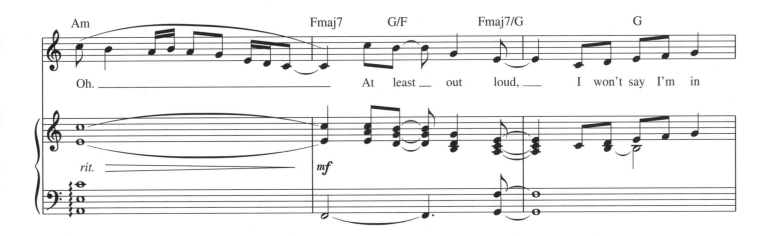

# THE PAST IS ANOTHER LAND

## from Elton John and Tim Rice's *Aida*

Music by Elton John
Lyrics by Tim Rice

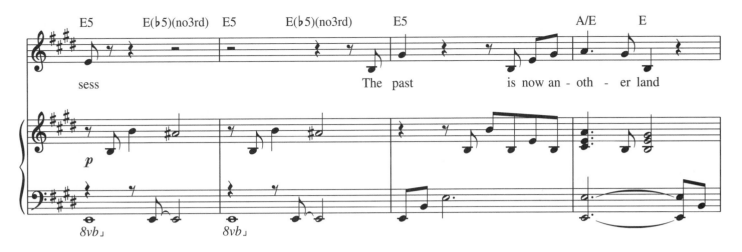

sess                    The past    is now an - oth - er land

far be-yond my ___ reach ___    In - vad - ed by    in - sid-ious    for - eign

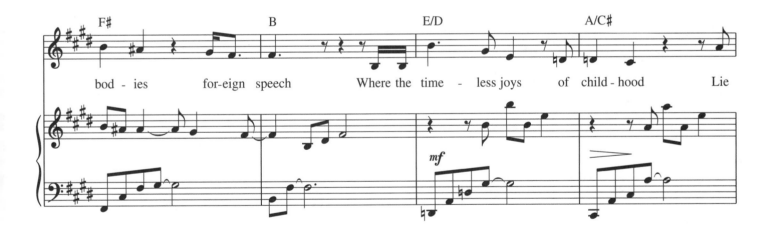

bod - ies    for-eign speech    Where the time - less joys    of child - hood    Lie

bro - ken on    the beach ___                                                    The

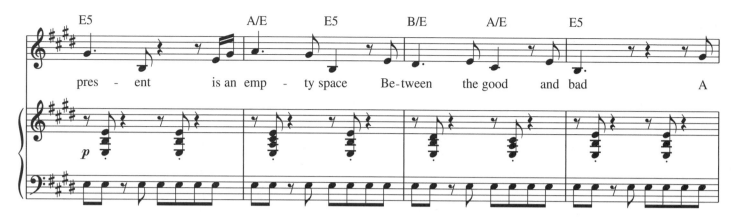

pres - ent is an emp - ty space Be-tween the good and bad A

mo - ment lead - ing no - where Too point - less to be sad __ But

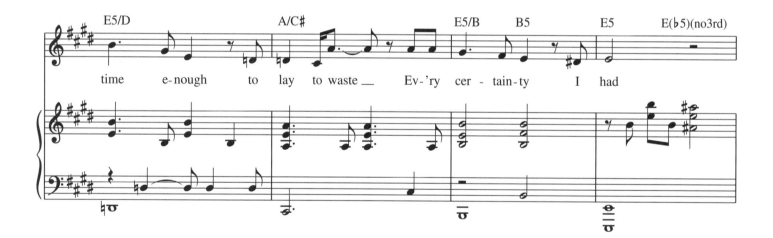

time e-nough to lay to waste __ Ev-'ry cer - tain-ty I had

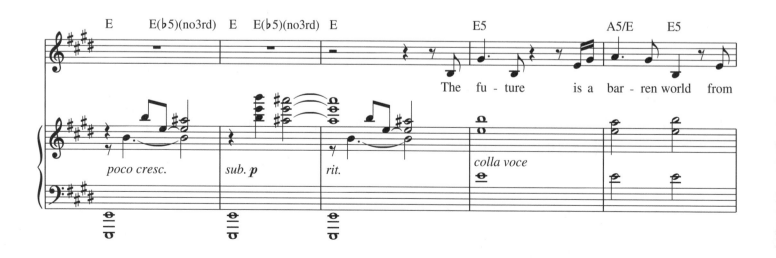

The fu - ture is a bar - ren world from

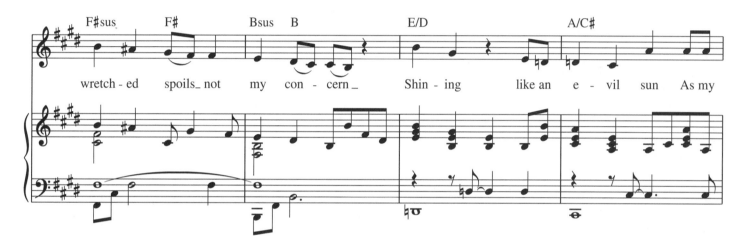

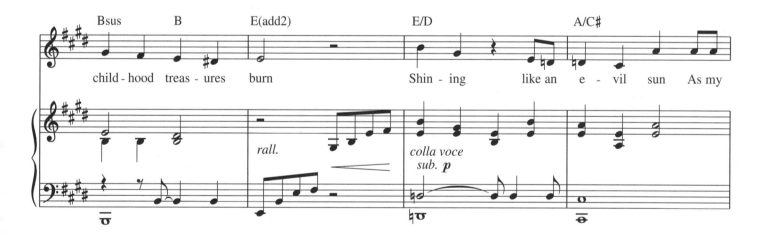

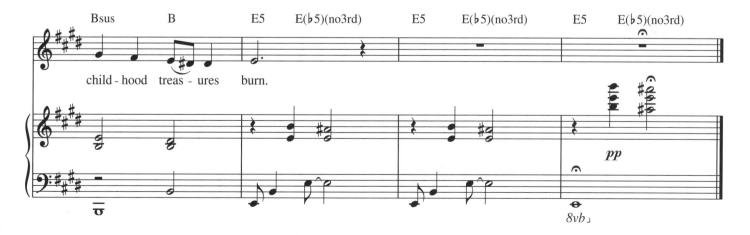

# BOP TO THE TOP
## from the Disney Channel Original Movie *High School Musical*

Words and Music by Randy Petersen
and Kevin Quinn

**Latin dance groove**

I be-lieve in dream - ing, ___

shoot-ing for the stars. ___ Ba - by, to ___ be num - ber one, ___ you've

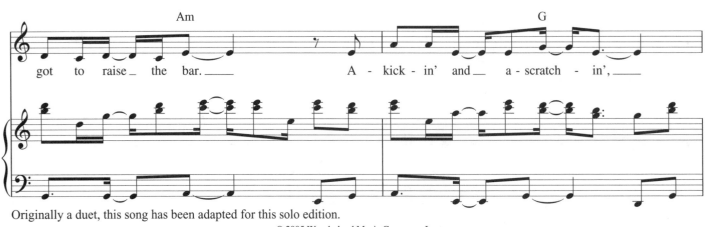

got to raise ___ the bar. ___ A - kick - in' and ___ a - scratch - in', ___

Originally a duet, this song has been adapted for this solo edition.

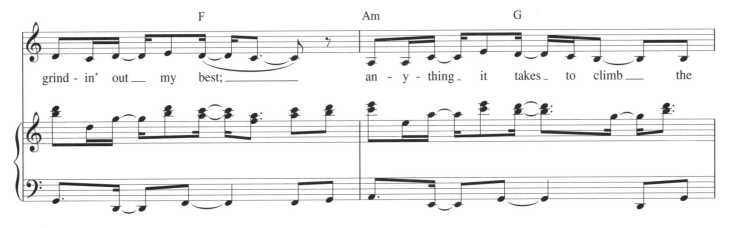

grind - in' out __ my best; _____ an - y - thing __ it takes __ to climb __ the

lad - der of __ suc - cess. Work our tails __ off ev - 'ry day; __

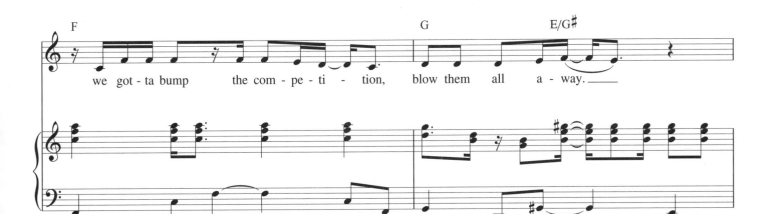

we got - ta bump the com - pe - ti - tion, blow them all a - way. ____

*Caliente!*      *Suave!*      Yeah, we're gon - na bop, bop, bop, bop to the top;

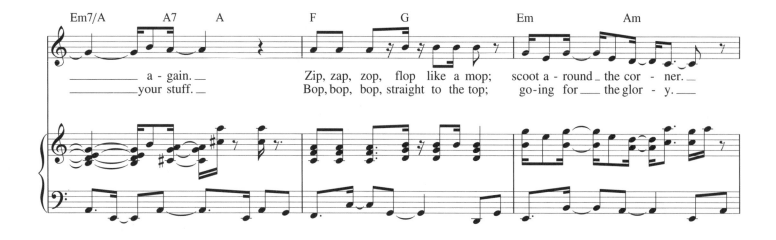

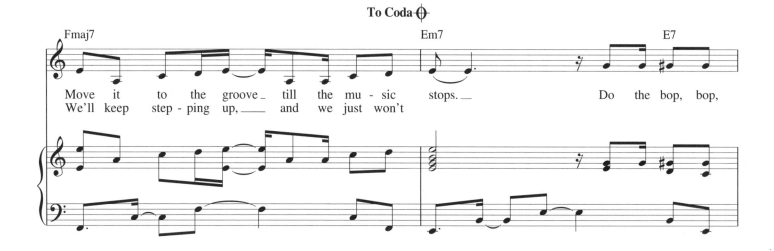

Gim-me, gim-me; shim-my, shim-my. Shake some boot - y and turn a - round.

Flash a smile in their _ di - rec - tion.

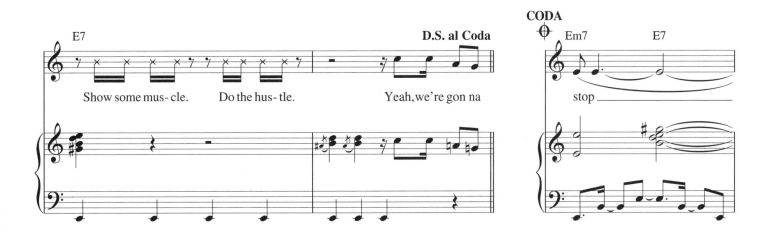

Show some mus- cle. Do the hus- tle. Yeah, we're gon na

stop _____

till we reach the top. _____ Bop to the top!

# BREAKING FREE

## from the Disney Channel Original Movie *High School Musical*

Words and Music by
JAMIE HOUSTON

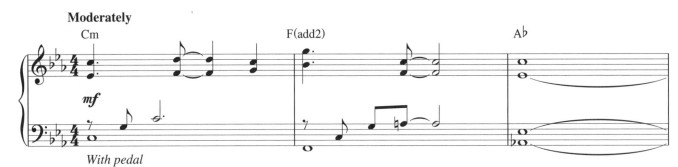

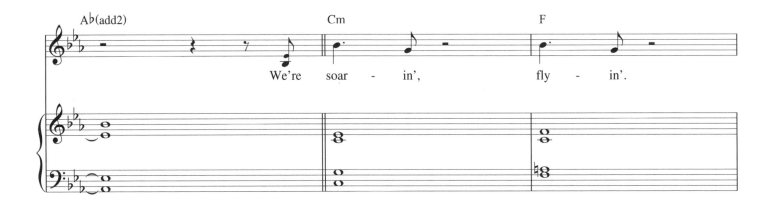

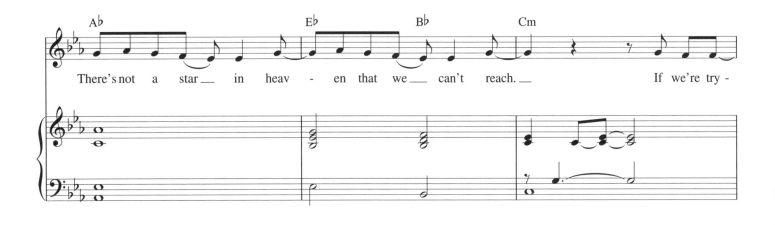

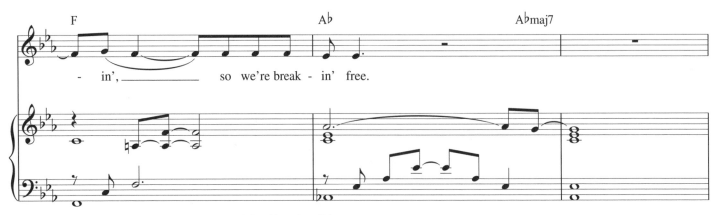

Originally a duet, this song has been adapted for this solo edition.

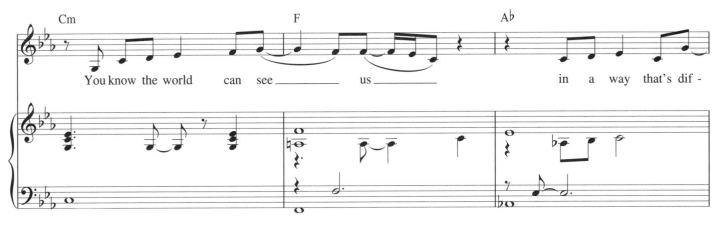

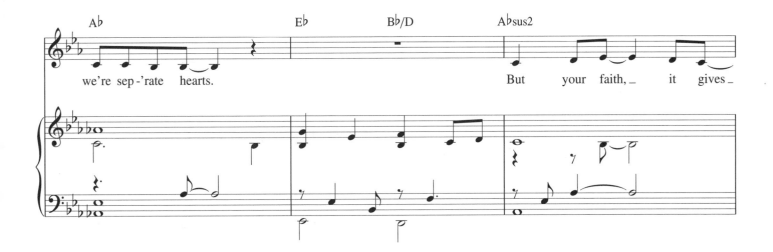

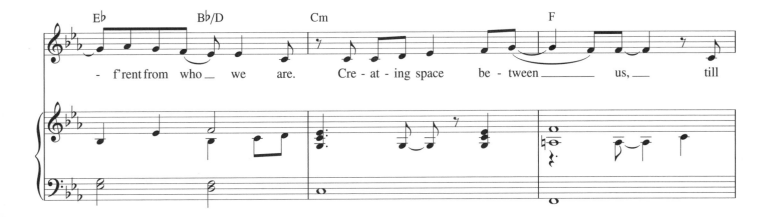

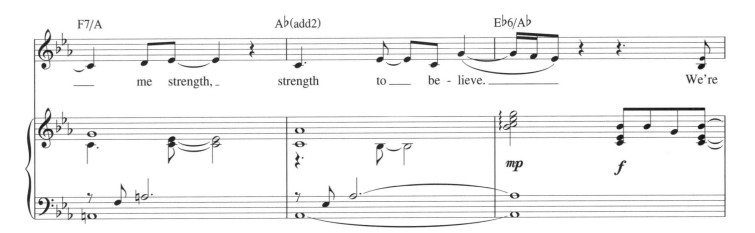

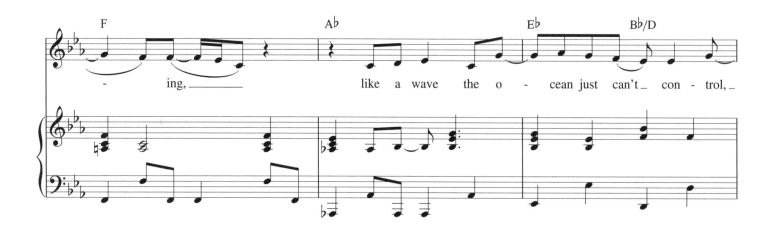

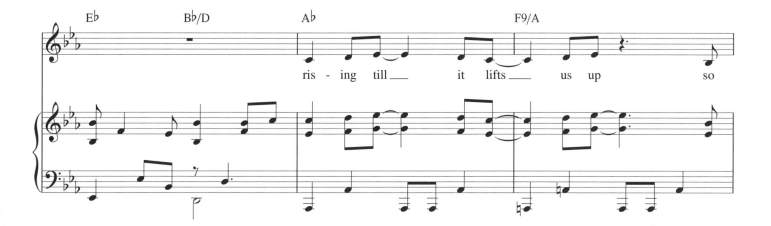

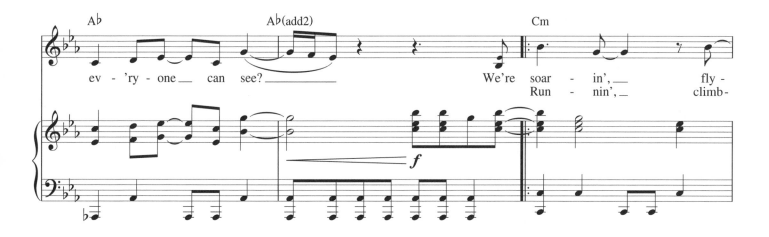

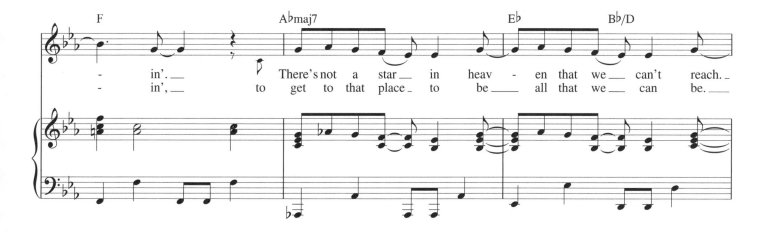

If we're try - in', __ yeah, we're break - in' free. Oh, we're break-
Now's the time, _____ so we're break - in' free. We're break-

1
in' free.

2
in' free. More than hope, more than faith,

this is truth, this is fate; and to - geth - er, we see ___

___ it com - in'. ___ More than you, more than me, not a want, but a need:

both of us break-in' free. ___ Soar - in', ___ fly -

- in'. ___ There's not a star ___ in heav - en that we ___ can't reach. ___

If we're try - in', yeah, we're break - in' free.

We're run - nin', ___ ooh, ___ climb - in' _____ to

get to the place _ to be _ all that we _ can be. _ Now's the time, _

_____ so we're break - in' free.

You know the world can see _____ us ___ in a way that's

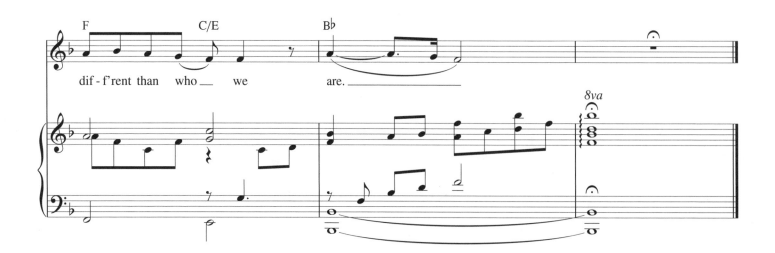

dif - f'rent than who _ we are. _____

# START OF SOMETHING NEW

## from the Disney Channel Original Movie *High School Musical*

Words and Music by Matthew Gerrard
and Robbie Nevil

Originally a duet, this song has been adapted for this solo edition.

never be-lieved in _____ what I could-n't see. _____ I nev-er

o-pened my heart _____ to all the pos-si-bil-i-ties. _____ Oh, _____ I

know that some-thing has changed; _____ nev-er felt this way. _____ { And right here to-night, _____ { I know it for real: _____

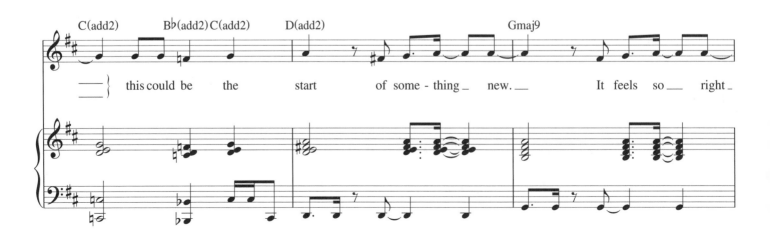

_____ } this could be the start of some-thing _____ new. _____ It feels so _____ right _____

to be here with __ you, __ oh. __ And now, look-ing in your __ eyes, __

**To Coda** ⊕

__ I feel in my heart __ the start of some-thing new. __

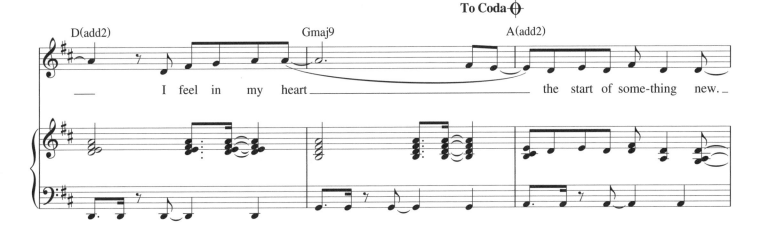

Now who'd-'ve ev - er thought that

we'd both be here __ to-night? __ Yeah, __ and the world __

**D(add2)** **Dsus2** **G(add2)/D**

looks so much bright - er, oh, __ with you by my __ side. ____

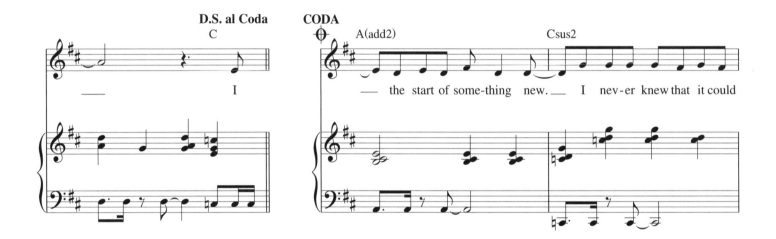

**D.S. al Coda** **CODA**
**C** **A(add2)** **Csus2**

__ I __ the start of some-thing new. __ I nev-er knew that it could

**G** **Bm7** **A(add2)** **A** **D**

hap-pen till it hap-pened to me. __ Oh, ____ yeah. ____

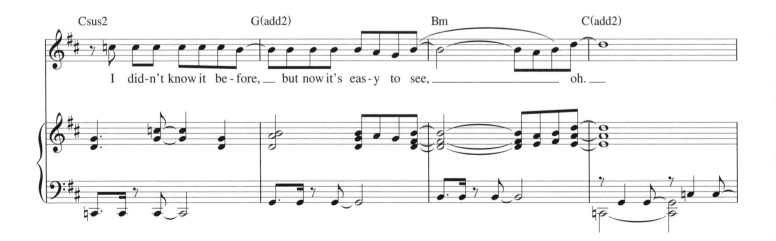

**Csus2** **G(add2)** **Bm** **C(add2)**

I did-n't know it be-fore, __ but now it's eas-y to see, ____ oh. __

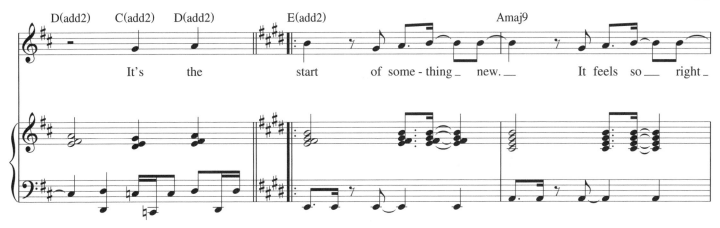

It's the start of some-thing _ new. _ It feels so _ right _

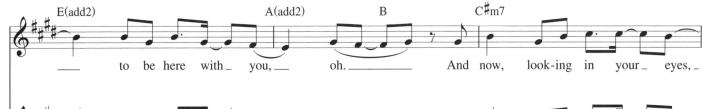

_ to be here with _ you, _ oh. _____ And now, look-ing in your _ eyes, _

_ I feel in my heart _____ that it's the

_ the start of some-thing new, _ ...the start of some thing new.

# WHAT I'VE BEEN LOOKING FOR

from the Disney Channel Original Movie *High School Musical*

Words and Music by Andy Dodd
and Adam Watts

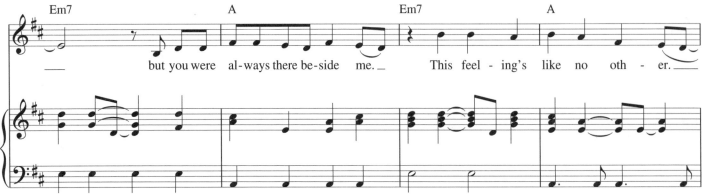

Originally a duet, this song has been adapted for this solo edition.

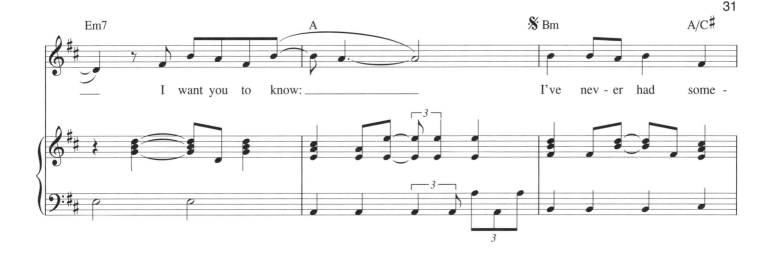

I've been look-ing for. _____

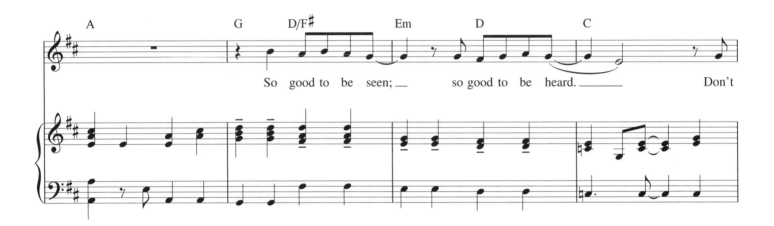

So good to be seen; ___ so good to be heard. _____ Don't

have to say a word. _____ For so long, I was lost; ___ so good to be found. __

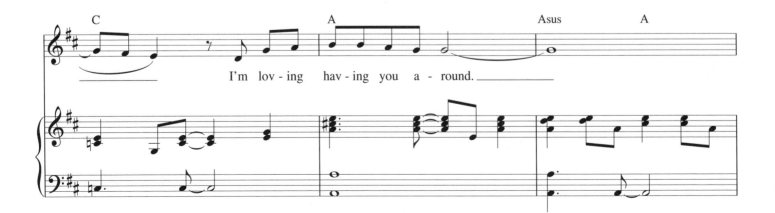

_____ I'm lov-ing hav-ing you a-round. _____

This feel-ing's like no oth - er.___ I want you to know:___

D.S. al Coda

**CODA**

I've been look-ing for.___ Doo doo doo, doo doo doo doo doo

doo; a - whoa, oh, oh, oh.___ whoa, oh, oh, oh.___

# WHEN THERE WAS ME AND YOU

from the Disney Channel Original Movie *High School Musical*

Words and Music by
Jamie Houston

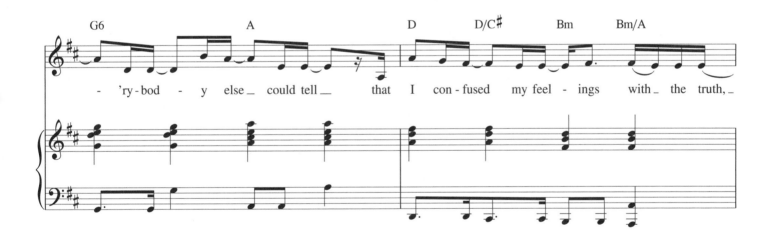

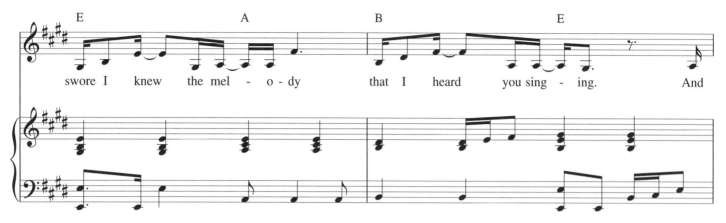

swore I knew the mel - o - dy that I heard you sing - ing. And

when you smiled,_ you made_ me feel_ like I could sing_ a - long._____ But then_

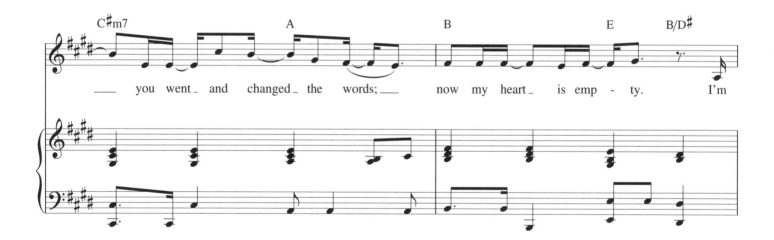

___ you went_ and changed_ the words;___ now my heart_ is emp - ty. I'm

on - ly left_ with used - to - be's_ and once up - on_ a song._ Now, I know_

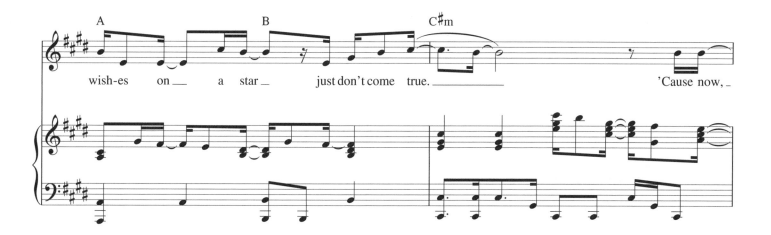

I can't be-lieve __ that I could be __ so blind. __ It's like you were float-

-ing while __ I was fall - ing, and I did n't mind, ___

be-cause I liked __ the view, ___ ooh. __

___ I thought you felt __ it too, __ when there was me __ and you.

# BREAKAWAY
## from *The Princess Diaries 2: Royal Engagement*

Words and Music by Bridget Benenate,
Avril Lavigne and Matthew Gerrard

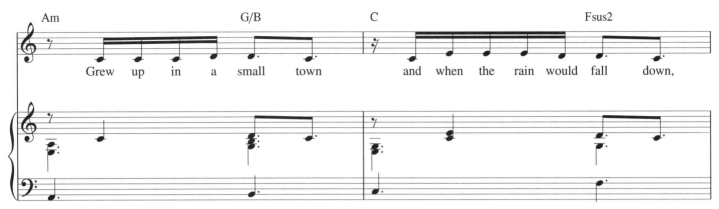

Am     G/B     C     Fsus2

Grew up in a small town     and when the rain would fall down,

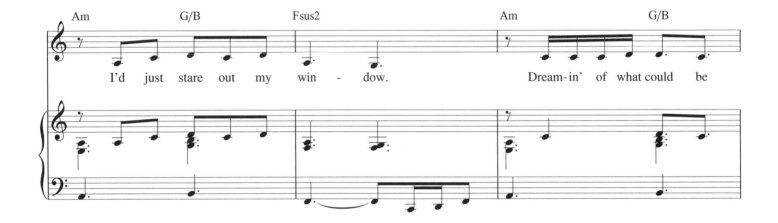

Am     G/B     Fsus2     Am     G/B

I'd just stare out my win - dow.     Dream-in' of what could be

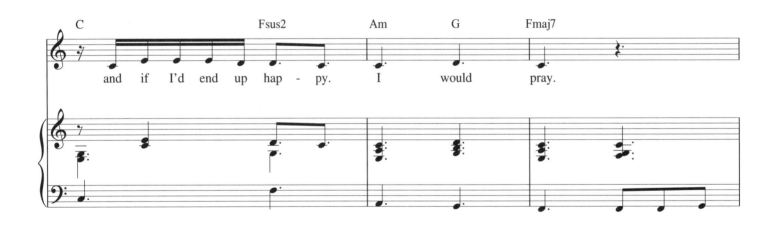

C     Fsus2     Am     G     Fmaj7

and if I'd end up hap - py.     I would pray.

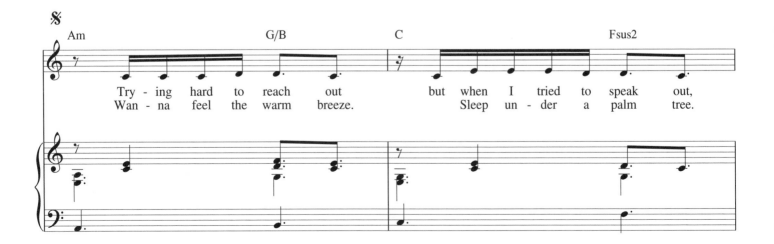

Am     G/B     C     Fsus2

Try - ing hard to reach out     but when I tried to speak out,
Wan - na feel the warm breeze.     Sleep un - der a palm tree.

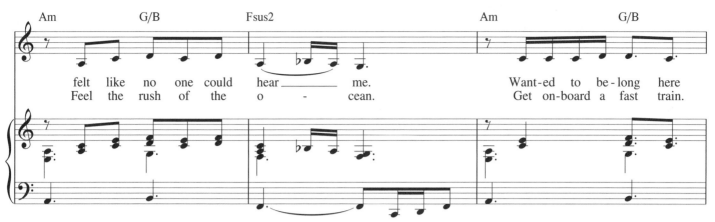

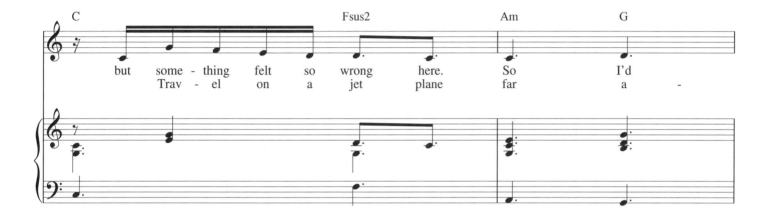

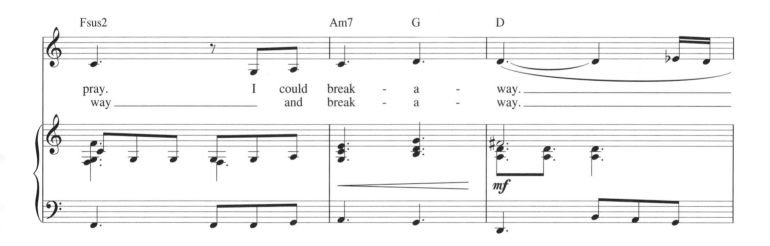

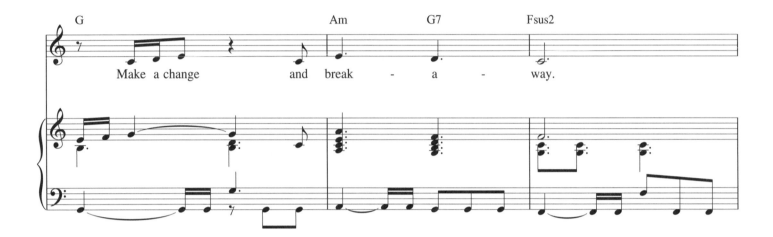

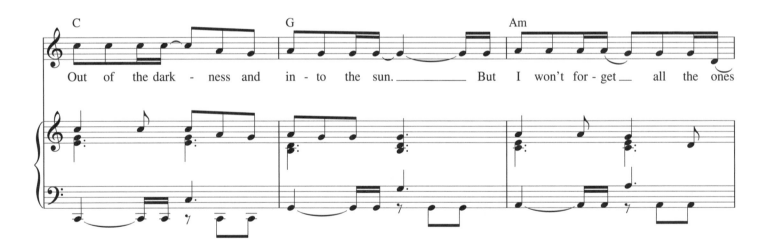

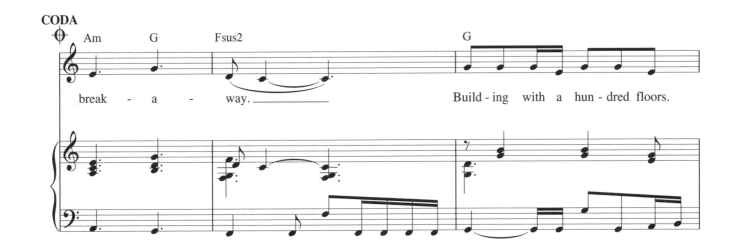

got-ta keep mov-in' on, mov-in' on. Fly a - way, break-a-

way._____ I'll spread my wings and I'll learn how to fly.__

Though it's not eas-y to tell__ you good-bye, got-ta take a risk. Take a chance.

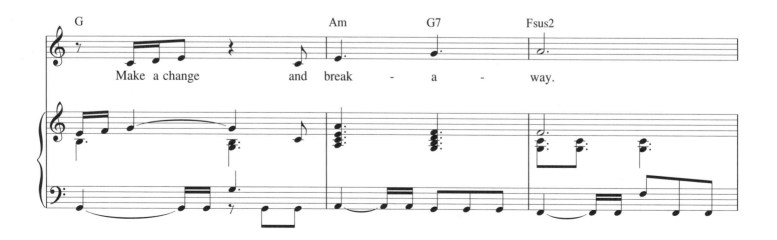

Make a change and break - a - way.

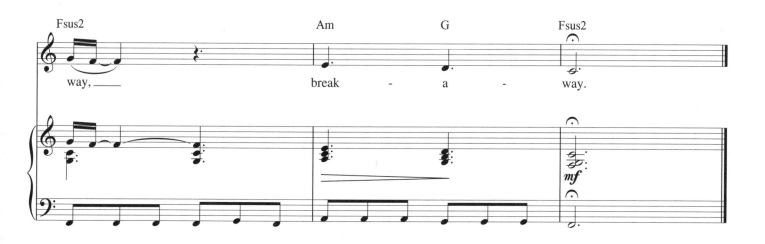

# CAN YOU FEEL THE LOVE TONIGHT

from Walt Disney Pictures' *The Lion King*

Music by Elton John
Lyrics by Tim Rice

**Pop Ballad**

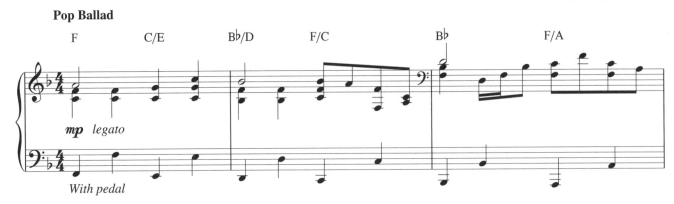

There's a calm __ sur - ren - der
There's a time __ for ev - 'ry - one,

to the rush __ of day, __ when the heat __ of the roll - ing world __
if they on - ly learn __ that the twist - ing ka - lei - do - scope __

can be turned __ a - way. __ An en - chant - ed mo - ment,
moves us all __ in turn. __ There's a rhyme __ and rea - son

and it sees___ me through.___ It's e - nough___ for this rest - less war - rior
to the wild___ out - doors ___ when the heart___ of this star - crossed voy - ag - er

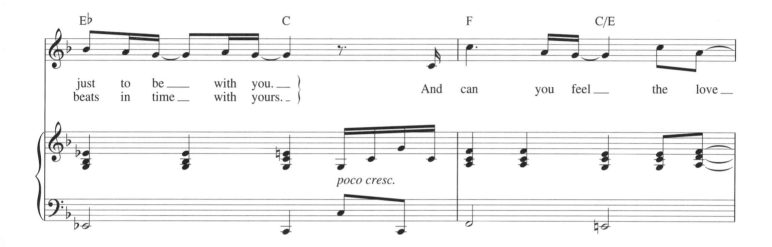

just to be ___ with you. ___  And can you feel ___ the love ___
beats in time ___ with yours. ___

*poco cresc.*

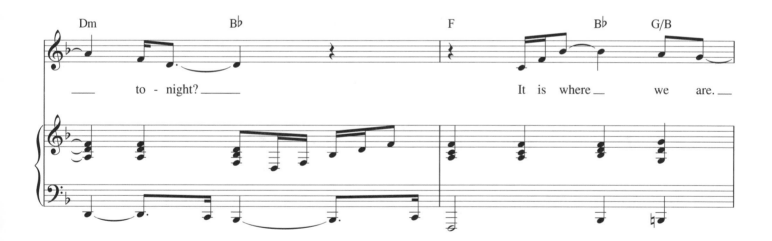

___ to - night? _____ It is where ___ we are. ___

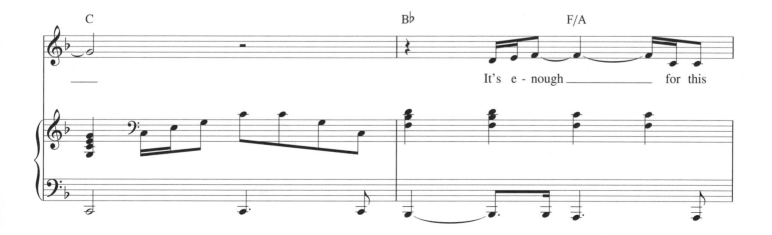

___  It's e - nough _____ for this

wide - eyed \_\_\_ wan - der - er        that    we    got    this    far. \_\_\_

\_\_\_        And    can    you    feel \_\_\_    the    love \_\_\_

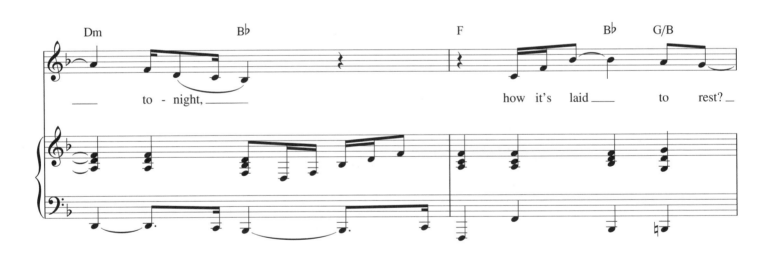

\_\_\_        to - night, _____        how    it's    laid \_\_\_    to    rest? \_\_\_

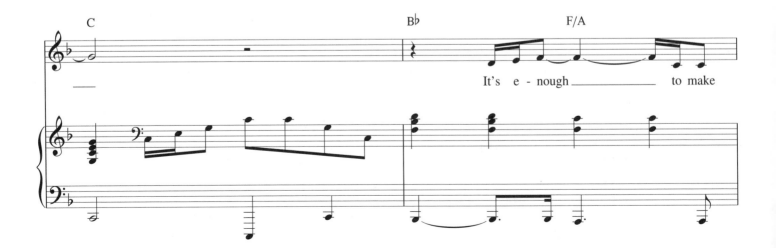

\_\_\_        It's    e - nough _____    to    make

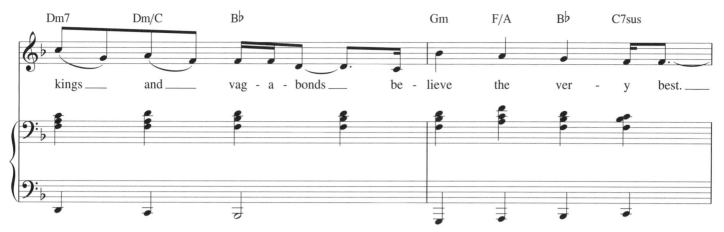

kings ___ and ___ vag - a - bonds ___ be - lieve the ver - y best. ___

*poco dim.*

It's e - nough ___ to make

kings ___ and ___ vag - a - bonds ___ be - lieve the ver - y best. ___

*rall.*

*molto rit.*

# REFLECTION
## from Walt Disney Pictures' *Mulan*

Music by Matthew Wilder
Lyrics by David Zippel

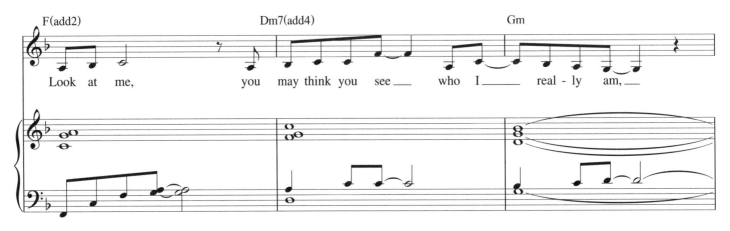

Look at me, you may think you see who I real-ly am,

but you'll nev-er know me. Ev-'ry day it's as if I play a part.

Now I see if I wear a mask I can fool the world, but I can-not fool my
But some-how I will show the world what's in-side my heart and be loved for who I

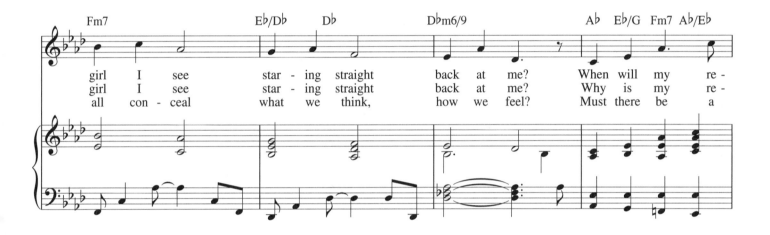

*I forced I don't know? Must I won't hide? pre- pre-*

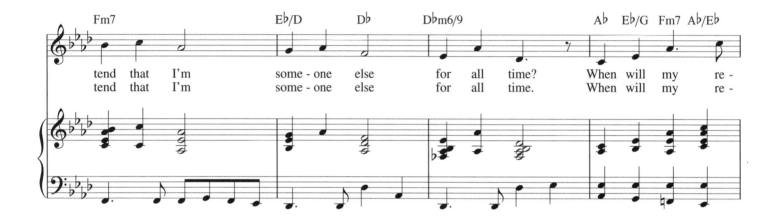

*tend that I'm some - one else for all time? When will my re-*
*tend that I'm some - one else for all time. When will my re-*

**To Coda** ⊕

*flec - tion show who I am? __ In - side, __ there's a*
*flec - tion show*

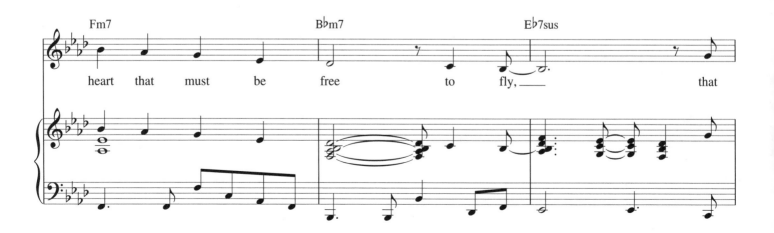

*heart that must be free to fly, ___ that*

burns with a need to know the rea - son why.

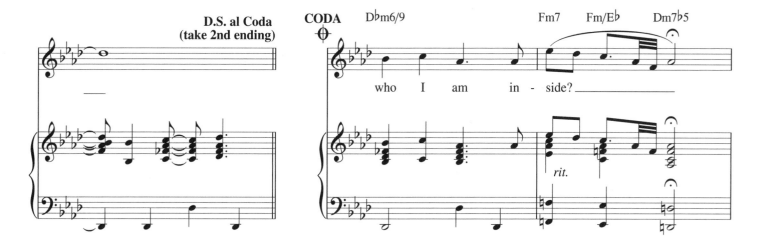

**D.S. al Coda**
**(take 2nd ending)**

**CODA**

who I am in - side?

When will my re - flec - tion show who I am in -

*a tempo*

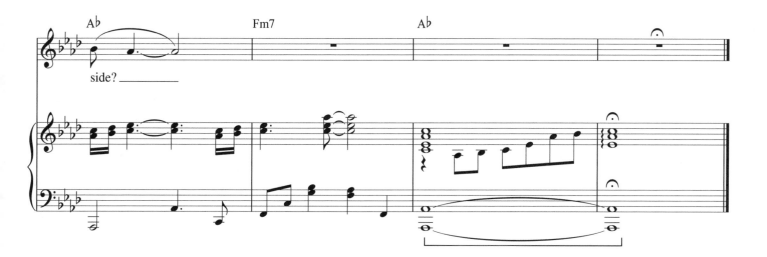

side?

# About the Enhanced CD

In addition to full performances and piano accompaniments playable on both your CD player and computer, this enhanced CD also includes tempo adjustment and transposition software for computer use only. This software, known as the Amazing Slow Downer, was originally created for use in pop music to allow singers and players the freedom to independently adjust both tempo and pitch elements. Because we believe there may be valuable educational use for these features in classical and theatre music, we have included this software as a tool for both the teacher and student. For quick and easy installation instructions of this software please see below.

This new software feature allows you to adjust the tempo up and down without affecting the pitch. Likewise, the Amazing Slow Downer allows you to shift pitch up and down without affecting the tempo. We recommend that these new tempo and pitch adjustment features be used with care and insight. Ideally, you will be using these recorded accompaniments and the Amazing Slow Downer for practice only.

The audio quality may be somewhat compromised when played through the Amazing Slow Downer. This compromise in quality will not be a factor in playing the CD audio track on a normal CD player or through another audio computer program.

Installation instructions for the Amazing Slow Downer software:

## For Macintosh OS 8, 9 and X:
- Load the CD-ROM into your CD-ROM Drive on your computer.
- Each computer is set up a little differently. Your computer may automatically open the audio CD portion of this enhanced CD and begin to play it.
- Double-click on the data portion of the CD-ROM (which will have the Hal Leonard icon in red and be named as the book).
- Double-click on the "Amazing OS 8 (9 or X)" folder.
- Double-click "Amazing Slow Downer"/"Amazing X PA" to run the software from the CD-ROM, or copy this file to your hard disk and run it from there.
- Follow the instructions on-screen to get started. The Amazing Slow Downer should display tempo, pitch and mix bars. Click to select your track and adjust pitch or tempo by sliding the appropriate bar to the left or to the right.

## For Windows:
- Load the CD-ROM into your CD-ROM Drive on your computer.
- Each computer is set up a little differently. Your computer may automatically open the audio CD portion of this enhanced CD and begin to play it.
- To access the CD-ROM features, click on My Computer then right click on the Drive that you placed the CD in. Click Open. You should then see a folder named "Amazing Slow Downer". Click to open the "Amazing Slow Downer" folder.
- Double-click "setup.exe" to install the software from the CD-ROM to your hard disk. Follow the on-screen instructions to complete installation.
- Go to "Start", "Programs" and find the "Amazing Slow Downer" folder. Go to that folder and select the "Amazing Slow Downer" software.
- Follow the instructions on-screen to get started. The Amazing Slow Downer should display tempo, pitch and mix bars. Click to select your track and adjust pitch or tempo by sliding the appropriate bar to the left or to the right.
- Note: On Windows NT, 2000, XP and Vista the user should be logged in as the "Administrator" to guarantee access to the CD-ROM drive. Please see the help file for further information.

## Minimum system requirements:

### For Macintosh:

Power Macintosh; Mac OS 8.5 or higher; 4 MB Application RAM; 8x Multi-Session CD-ROM drive

### For Windows:
Pentium Processor; Windows 95, 98, ME, NT, 2000, XP, Vista; 4 MB Application RAM; 8x Multi-Session CD-ROM drive